(ADO)RATION

Novels
Pushing the Bear
The Only Piece of Furniture in the House
Flutie
Fuller Man

Stories
Trigger Dance
Firesticks
Monkey Secret
The Voice That Was in Travel

Essays
Claiming Breath
The West Pole
The Cold-and-Hunger Dance

Plays
War Cries

Poems
Offering
One Age in a Dream
Lone Dog's Winter Count
Iron Woman
Boom Town
Coyote's Quodlibet
Primer of the Obsolete

Anthologies
Braided Lives
Two Worlds Walking
Visit Teepee Town: Native Writings after the Detours

(ADO)RATION

Diane Glancy

Chax Press 1999

ISBN 0-925904-26-0

Acknowledgment to *The Colorado Review* for "You remember now;" *High Plains Literary Review* for "Air for Flute Stop;" *Black Bear* for "Father this is;" *Nimrod* for "The Buzz;" *New Letters, The Writer and Religion* Issue, for "There's a story;" *Telegraphy* for "Would It Seem Winter;" *flyway literary review, Native American* Issue, (Iowa State University) for "Theology of Deer" and "Shim;" *Agassiz Review* for "All Things Holy;" *Gryphon* for "Near Big Cabin, Oklahoma" and "Trees Anchored to the Thought of Winter;" *SAIL, Studies in American Indian Literature* for "Peeling Red Potatoes for the Pow-Wow Soup;" *Sucarnochee Review* for "Adoration of the Magi" and "The Revenant;" *Salmon Magazine* for "Buffalo Trip;" *Pacific Coast Journal* for "Praize the pronghorns of the ocean's head" (under the title, "Symphony No. 103 in E-flat, Franz Joseph Haydn"); *Green Mountains Review* for "Light Beneath the Skin;" *Anathema Review* for "*El Nacimiento*;" *The Oregon Review* for "You know the Indian;" *The Briar Cliff Review* for "Custer Nat'l Park;" *Peregrine* for "Walker Gallery, Minneapolis;" *Sheba Review* for "I didn't want to be with him" (under the title, "Letter to my Former Husband"); *Footwork: The Paterson Literary Review* for "Thc light of (ado)ration," "Swan's Life Span" and "The Speech;" *The National Federation of State Poetry Societies Prize Anthology* for "Waves in the Fold of the Lake;" *100 Words* (University of Iowa) for "The Dress;" *Akwe:-kon Journal* for "The light of (ado)ration," "Well you push your mind along the road," "Yo, Hopper, fragile as a bird" and "Assimilation."

"Ledger Book Drawing" and "Homage" appear in *Durable Breath: Contemporary Native American Poetry,* John E. Smelcer and D. L. Birchfield, editors, Salmon Run Press, Anchorage, Alaska.

"Light Beneath the Skin," "Theology of Deer" and "The Transformation Band" appear in *Odd Angels of Heaven,* Harold Shaw Publishers, Wheaton, Illinois.

I also thank the Jerome Foundation for a Travel Grant which made it possible to finish this manuscript.

Table of Contents

And Rebekah spoke to Jacob, her son, saying,

Behold, I heard your father speak to Esau, your brother, saying, Bring me some venison, and make me savory food, that I may eat, and bless you before the Lord before my death...

Now therefore, my son, obey my voice... Go now to the flock, and fetch me from there two good kids of the goats; and I will make the savory food for your father, such as he loves. And you shall bring it to your father, that he may eat, and bless you before his death.

And Jacob said to Rebekah, his mother,

Behold, Esau, my brother, is a hairy man, and I am smooth...

And [Rebekah] put the skins of the kids of the goats upon his hands, and upon the smooth of his neck...

And [Jacob] came unto his father, and said,

I am Esau, your first-born; I have done according as you bade me: sit, eat my venison, and bless me.

Genesis 27: 5-19

You know them by their stealing

by their will that says *I take*
by the God who brought them
(who had an eye like a suck hole
for what he wanted)

he wanted his people to have the land
(if they took from their own brother
they could take from anyone)

they came with their goats and lambs
their kneading troughs
their ragtime band.

Ledger Book Drawing

The Indian when he first drew a horse
riding into battle
drew the brave sidesaddle not knowing
how to draw a leg on the other side
of the horse. And both eyes on the
same side of the head. It was getting down
the visible parts
when invisible
they're still there.
The Indian knew it.
But not trusting something
not seen
to be there when needed
the Indian drew both legs both eyes
so the brave would have them
not leaving to chance
what he could see
how he could be assured.

Homage

It was not that we did not know \ the wagons \ in visions \ would cover the land. From ours was \ not theirs \ but how their lives spread. Wolves ran from \ trails of them. Buffalo \ soon on the ground. The blue coats \ horses of them \ worked \ later \ praises from our eyes. Seeing not anywhere \ that which they fought. Ours the opening \ the clouds over our heads topping. It was them who drove us \ first to paradise.

The Dress

I had a brown and yellow check dress, the checks close as screen
wire on the back door. At first, nothing could get through, not
the flat, heavy words, not the needle-shaped ones.
But they kept on
with Christ
chugging him across the prairie. *You're dark with sin*, they
said, *the savior will zip you through the light.* Each day
I stood in the door waiting for the cake they said they had.
I wanted the small totem-poles of wax, burning at the top,
a gift from the bees. Not until the sun stretched into
shadows, disappeared into dark, I ate the wax spots on my
dress, tasted the light from the hive.

You know the Indian

when he saw a man on a horse said *woah, a four-legged!* Six
really though two legs unusable because they were too
short. But *a four-legged with two hands two heads a mane
and amazing tail.* Then if that wasn't enough the creature
came apart from itself. Could actually dismount the other
in a truely emblamatic reference by which you discover the
binary trail you'll probably be on the rest of life. And you
saddle up.

As if
Jesus

on a motorcycle with an angel driving the sidecar. Yes, the
angel's hand raised as if riding the rodeo. Reaching
through a hole in the air and it's like putting your finger
into a light-socket and you're wired.

You bunny-hop
with the
Conquistadors

riding the horse up from Mexico being extinct on the
North American continent since the Ice Age now after
crossing on ships from *Espanola* they come back. Yup.
Maybe it's the speed of the Harley.
Maybe it's the bleeding-heart of Jesus flapping on his chest.
No t-shirt logo. No. Jesus is quick as a whip-tailed lizard.
You feel him running through your insides. Washing the
hurt. The mean-spirited stuff you've done. You remember
as a child you heard him rolling like a loose hub-cap. You
knew him in high school. Smoking with the gang in the
parking lot. You know how in those days you were always
drawn to the hoods.

Air for Flute Stop

This morning when there is no sleep
you pat white flour on your face
and cover your hair with lard
to hide its blackness.

Maybe under a bonnet of sleep
a flower pressed to your nose
you would know the fragrance
of the prairie more than this.

Faster than air freight
jazz movements of the plane's shadow
jangle over the earth.
Oh we stopped the migration of herds

nailed buffalo hooves to the ground
the arrow bent \ the bow string dangling
uncovered this sleep-wake \ *whoo bee do*
when flute is an airplane w/out wings.

There's a story

of a time of hunger when Jesus called a buffalo across Geronimo's path, and Geronimo shot his arrow into the buffalo and cut out the liver and ate it, and when Jesus came to eat with Geronimo, he looked at the arrow swift as lightning into the heart and said, *where's the liver of this buffalo?* And Geronimo said, *it didn't have one*, and Jesus said, *man that was strange.* And when Geronimo got hungry again, Jesus said, *there wasn't any liver in that buff? No*, Geronimo told him. And when the tribe cried for buffalo meat, Jesus asked again if there was a liver. *No*, Geronimo said, and sat on the hill looking for buffalo. Well, Jesus let him go a few more days, then asked one last time if that buffalo had a liver. And Geronimo with his tribe depending on him and all, still said, *no.* And Jesus said, *I'll make a pasture for them in all the open ranges of the heavens. Where the grass is red. The sky, violet. The teepees, turquoise. I will give them bows and arrows and buffalo without number, and all of them, without livers.*

Well you push your mind along the road

when there is no road over the field then you lift your voice
and say *praise to you nothing* and nothing begins to hear
and becomes prideful and before you know it nothing
becomes something at first maybe just a foot-print in the
dust at the side of the road then you find a piece of fur and
a few bones from the last meal then *whizzo* you see a
shadow dart between the bushes and you catch glimpses
out of the side of your eye and you see a falling star or a
heads-up penny and you know it will happen and you keep
saying praise and soon you're sure there's something where
nothing was. In fact it's not long before
                                        there's enough
                                        of something
                                        that there's
a confrontation of wills
a split in understanding
that penetrates to the very nature of being
a scale of epistemology
metaphysical or something like that
and you're arguing with something
to establish your being
by the very disruption and opposition
to the other
finally even you're on a migration
which is later called slippage between self
and other
or summer to winter camp
and you feel like a codefendant
in the world and you have another being
you have to struggle
to bring into understanding
all over again.

Yo, Hopper, fragile as a bird

The sparrows ate the seed I threw out. The grackles chased them away and ate their seed. The bluejays chased the grackles away and ate their seed. And he did nothing! Nothing. I tell you. Why didn't he go out and kick tail-feather? And tell the oppressor they are standing on the terrace of their next lives. It was then I saw the sparrows riding the backs of angels as they grazed the open fields under heaven. *We are waiting for our Father to say we can come. A trip we wait for, dreaming the bluejays will be too large for the trip. Too large for the needle's eye.*

Trees Anchored to the Thought of Winter in the Apple Thinning Moon

The denominations divided the tribes
so they'd each have someone
in the winter before them
howling at Christ
showing they'd done the shepherding work
they'd done
on this dark earth
under the small white spittle of the moon.

They came with a Bible

saying it was all right to take.
Did not Jacob steal Esau's birthright?
Did not Israel enter Canaan?
Who was this God who allowed it?
We sat at the campground and talked.
We were supposed to say Jesus and know their God.
They baptized us as a sign
we'd been washed in the blood of the lamb.
We looked at the wagons going by,
wings folded over the wagon beds
saying, *holy holy,* to our death.
Their sacred ground was a building.
Didn't they know it was the grass under our feet
and the clouds above?
All the earth was holy.
A man could worship anywhere.
He could talk to the ancestors and spirits.
The animals— the grass eaters
and those four-leggeds who first tore the flesh,
drank the blood.

Peeling Red Potatoes for the Pow-Wow Soup

The dull knife scrapes the skin
with the sound of a bird disturbed
over some intrusion
or the sound of cardboard we sledded downhill.
There's an Indian legend
of the stars as holes in the night sky
to let the other world shine through.
I remember once my brother
stepped on a flower pot in the basement.
It broke and he fell on it
cutting the back of his leg
to the white fat underneath.
It's the spirit world just under the skin,
the spirit world above the tarp of sky.
I felt it when rage passed over our house
like new paint.
Somehow the boards held together
and we were clean.
There must be no boundary
between spirit and self,
no distance more than a crawl space
from the (ado)ring light.

The Speech

From a boat no less
he spoke to the multitudes
in globes of light
as if under a sunroof
in an auditorium,
waves sloping toward the stage.
How could the single trajectory
of his voice
disperse to everyone's center
at once?
The quiescent sea,
the glass of its mullioned waves,
the effect of light
rationing the sound?
He spoke in parables
as if all else wasn't enough
to mask the message,
the true meaning,
the whole universe full of riddles.
Birds carrying his voice
like seed?
Were they then silent too
so one voice on a ship in the water
could be divided
among the many on shore?
So many they pushed him
to the ship in the first place
where he now spoke,
as if a microphone in a lasso
around his neck
so the select could hear,
could be explained to,
the score.
The nonlinear conditions

of the game.
Its perimeters on the sea
calm as slate that day
not unsteadied by motion.
The wind quitting its fanning duties
so one voice
could project faith
that small, nonrational thing.

Father this is

no resting ground you gave me
this long flight across the plains
I feel arrival now
to get off this journey
from the pines
the rain storms above rivers
higher than before
I take the bones
the large bird's foot
father
the *maple leafs*
of your dead hands.

All Things Holy

Back in the landscape I worshipped
the '39 Dodge crawled off to the stockyards
each day with my father in it.
I remember the roar
when he backed the car
from the basement garage
on cold mornings.
Sometimes he only got half-way up
the steep drive
and would have to let it roll back down
under the house
where he'd rev it up again.
I watched it bolt from the chute
from the window of my bedroom over the drive.
I listened to the wild snorting
from under my room.
Then the blue dodge was bull,
growling fiercely, pawing the ground.
Sometimes I slept in the attic
and from there
the drive was even farther down.
On dark mornings
the car transformed under the stars
above the basement garage.
I longed to leap to the heavens
I had prowled before my birth.
I don't know why he didn't back the car
into the garage
and get a running start up the steep drive.
It only wanted to be free
maybe the way stars secretly long
not to be our guides
with such authority
as we give the poor fixed beasts.

Would It Seem Winter

Your (ado)ration is
the cattle
you em(bell)ish

the s(lit) throat
you interpolate
as (ado)ring
wound

you improv-
the scrape
of hide

drive
cows from
their
trans(form)ment
con(fined).

Shim

You gave me a practical
life not to think of it in
those terms but this
off-side feeling I still have.
Hairy father at your sawbuck in the
steep basement
after hunting you bring
back pheasant
pluck off their feathers
on the floor.
I touch the blue shriveled holes
where the metal pellets went in.
In the woods the saw-whet hoots
its eye like eyes on
the rocking horse
you made for me
threw away the feathers when I wanted them
begged for them to make wings.
Above our yard
trees yield their hard brown fruit
the coralberry of my breasts
which never swelled
and hair grew
which cut like sawgrass
when I shaved the sea under our house.
I was neither son
nor daughter to you
old Noah
as I collected the sad
little droppings of pheasants.
I was shim
a small wood wedge
between you and our ark
when it stopped on Ararat.
Father at your sawbuck and level

its bubble to one side
the color of a urine specimen
from someone who is sick
out where dog stars bark
from the high fence of their pen
and the ark sits straight
on its mountainside.

The Revenant

The landscape meshes past.
The reflected one slower
from its point of departure on the window
of the bus.
The real one
passing through the glass.
The night we stood
at my father's bed,
my brother watching
our reflection on the window.
The fields plod their way
behind the barn.
The pines there trollop
to keep the furrows from raking up
the way he tried to leave the bed
until the needle pricked
that kept his muscles from moving.
One landscape taking off over the other
the way memory unfolds.
The clutch popping in the old Dodge
on the hill from our house.
The measure of faith it took
to get to the old place
down through the winding hills
below Missouri.
The jars hanging on fences
like those at his hospital bed.
My brother and I in the backseat
crossing that invisible line
and he lifting his hand,
trying to turn to the backseat
to hit us in the head.
The trees lifted
separate from one another,
the slower ones on the bus window

turning past the faster ones
through the glass.
How his face
looked like his Indian mother's that night
as though fighting against this last trip
she turned saying, *behave now,*
here, give me your hand.
The white line from other side of the road
fencing the ditch through the glass.
The old hospital room war-dancing
over the fields,
my brother watching the image of my mother
at the foot of the bed,
the minister beside her saying
soon my father would know
what we've been wondering.
The fields passing
in overlaps at different paces.
The bus stopping now at Mason City.
The pockets of grief that open
now and then
sweeping away roads in spring floods.
The bus window
stretched like a rubberband.
The brightness centering through glass.
My father's mother
waiting somewhere.
Finally she could come for him.
The bus pulling onto the road
tossing us,
his hand jerking in reflex action
turning back to life
one last time
letting go.

Resurrection

You see him *levitational,* herding buffalo on their migra-
tion to the stockyards, saying, *it will be all right, we're*
driving a divided highway into the after-life. But his arms
are crossed, some bright *moonthing,* a parachute behind his
head. He leads another herd up the chute
                                                            you see him
                                                            without mercy
in a blood-red poncho over the leafless land.

Crossing Wyoming

It was worse than we imagined
as if no one had been there
as though it didn't exist
with clear roads under sunlight
but a haze we had to hack at
worse than old places we carry
there's nothing like driving
on the road all day
at night our feet still climb
taking folds of a map
as the final reference point
upstairs we touch the snow
poking tunnels with our fingers
pines pressed through
like a winter scene on white felt
stored in the attic
jagged mountains of rainspots
on a Teton blue wall.

Yellowstone

Flicker of sun through the pines.
Towering points
pointing to the sky.
Strings of snow
like smoke from mountain cabins
far back.
None of the missing elements
without reminders
something we boarded up
years ago
still leaking.

Buffalo Trip

Now after a long time
the clouds hang their blanket
the sort of jerga weave you see in museums
the Sunday afternoon before you start back.
Under the Montana sky
the wind you know
making a tromp to an outpost on the horizon.
If you're not hearing the proper intention
the reason you're gathering
in the buffalo section and it's nearly
four on an afternoon when warm is
just now selling books
in back of a crowded store
shelves up to the ceiling
and a door propped open to let in a little air
and in the heat rising
and dust from the outskirts
you see insects look like small buffalo
with wings
circling near the ceiling and ladders where
they step to heaven
and now back without apparent tools.
You hear them speak about the hunting grounds
they've seen no doubt.
They talk about the moon as a flue cover
in an old bunkhouse.
You think of the livestock yards where your father worked.
You think now you see him in his hat. The one you wore as
a small girl when they took your picture with it down over
your ears with your hand raised to find your way out but
you hear your father laughing and you know your mother
is taking your picture and you hold still because there's
something about you they like.

And the buffalo talk about how in the hereafter they don't feel arrows in their backs. They don't feel flies. If anyone in earshot would hear the sun rounding the corner. You find another turn-around on the Montana road though it's hard with the outposts you couldn't reach though your life depended on it. But once you do the place offers the sort of rough-hewn jerga weave used for saddle-blankets, ponchos and bunkhouse windows. Knowing the buffalo with their organization lobbying for grass-roots. You'd think the US army band or mere cavalry soldiers with tin plates riding the hips of their horses would give the buffalo a clue as to what would happen.

Custer Nat'l Park

I tell you we could hear the buffalo
eat grass.
They looked small as chickens
on the South Dakota knoll
but now close up
grass hangs from their mouths.
They stare back.
Ee hota.
The words not quite right
but anyway
we have so little time
before we leave our war cries.
Galloping faster
Custer Nat'l Park rallies like a streamer.
We flick the button to stop it from moving.
There are times I think
how the wilderness is a wool sweater
dried on high
when cleaners are called for in the label
at the back of the neck.
What there is to pick up
is a continual surprise.
In the souvenir shop
it's equal rain among the herds.
Yet a glimmer
hope makes
along the road sometimes
boarded with maybe a name barely visible.
The windmills of the plains we rifle past.
Their slippage into the next world
despite wind-speed all day.
Streams of it past the tourist stops.
The barns farther along the road.
The McCormick and Deering tractor.
The sky's white eggs.

Waves in the Fold of the Lake

Maybe the knowledge of how it would be
against the now of a warm afternoon
in October.
The silver maple in the backyard,
not silver really, but gray-barked
along the trunk. The leaves bright red.
You see them move sometimes.
Before the sky slips into the dark.
By daylight you're still watching leaves over
the roof of your house.
Sweeping now all day. Saying who needs
them anymore with winter at hand?
And how coming in the house among the baskets
hanging in the kitchen
you jar them with the broom-handle.
They rock like boats on the ceiling.

Or how the crowded afternoon is all
the more fast
because of the ones coming after it
like waves pushing Tenkiller's shore.
Even now the breath of wind moves the leaves
to the steep stairs
the sky spirits polish with wax.
You've heard stories of them. All the time.
Like the leaves they say are always red
but the sun for a while keeps them green.
And suddenly you'll find your feet on the stairs.
But now the day's yours to sweep
because you know the leaves won't be there long
and you'll outlast them chances are.
Yes, that's the way it is. The calm surface of the yard.
The sky spirits waiting.
Overhead.

Near Big Cabin, Oklahoma

The truck you wait for passes
now we follow
closely
all I can see
is the back of the shiny truck
for miles
it is the pursuit you know
your father tracking
his sales route
now you
a row of cemetery
stones like gulls
that inhabit
the lake country
we seem clipped and pasted here
nothing before us
but the silver flicker
of the screen.

Ration

Maybe our faces gradually turn into the white petal of a
petunia
fragile as distance
a tablecloth
an allotment
you know
eggless cakes
the war when it's over
a reservation road
a dusty field.

Assimilation

Tell me, if the Virgin Mary has walked throughout all the land, why has she never entered the wigwam of the Apache?
— Cochise

The land divided now by roads \
the rusted leaves \ fly.
Lightning frantic as limbs. Some upstairs woods
\ we aim for. Field trampled
by hooves of cattle \ glint of barn \
the gusty star flung as a javelin.

Adoration of the Magi, Jan Bruegel

A crowd in Bethlehem. The mere numbering of them in census time. The throngs under the gouge of light, a spat of candlewax on the vault of heaven. The focal point of Magi. Then Mary and the Child. Even the dogs, the wagon wheel, the heart-shaped rope in the corner. And behind them, the streams of people across the aqueduct to Bethlehem, looking more like Detroit, knowing or not knowing there was a Christ child in the manger and Mary whimpled as a nun. And where is Joseph? Is that him at the corner of the barn in his carpenter's apron talking to soldiers? His augers, reamers, awls, by the tree? The hatchet and Michigan ax? What of this kink in his plans? This setting up shop on the road and more of it ahead. The Y-support for the manger and its beam, the cross Joseph wouldn't live to see. How much didn't he understand there by the piles of straw, more of it than he wanted to see. The willet and barn hens. The accruals of halberds, blades, the salubrious bow of the Magi with their Florida water and frankincense. All of us later could talk of it. Long Sunday afternoons. And those on plow-seats across America's fields. The Euclidian planes of yards hedged with *blue girl* holly. Or maybe the crowds are the masses that would seek the Christ as though this fine earth were something that needed a way out. Once ice fishing in Minnesota, a shiner minnow on the end of a line, I watched the Y-forked vein on my hand. The brown star beside it. The wind is more than it is at 2 below. It can turn fingers into black worms. The landscape into hard fruit ripe with achenes unwilling to break. The lesser painter to Pieter, his father, of Flanders still, with the same translucent verdure of the sky. Even the rope for the woodcutter's ball, the horses, soldiers in helmets, the barn hens and lacewings. The flight to Egypt still ahead, the salvific cross, the fishing scenes after resurrection when the disciples would catch nothing and the Christ baby in the painting with his hand nearly raised, as if saying, already, *cast your net on the other side.*

Praize the pronghorns of the ocean's head

Praize the ear
which is the handle on the lid of the jar
of the head
praize the hymn
its snaily pace
the notes of boats upturned and down
across the staves
praize the beacon of the farmyard pine
praize Christ as overhead of the Church
the angels who are really leaves
they are so many in the yard
praize the five-below January morning
the atmosphere of ice
you start out
the sun-dog right there in the sky
its circle around the sun
a sacred shield
praizing the vessel's holy flight.

(Ado)ration

I could believe the Spirit-world moving the boundaries of its yard chairs. I could (ado)rate somewhat. But still it's hard to see the Great Spirit *white* as a sky on Sunday. The way the Apache speaks, he says a landscape, and someone knows he means the rocks by the ridge, and knows what happened there, and thereby knows the story the Apache tells. Likewise, the Spirit says, *Jerusalem*, he says, *Golgotha*, he says names like that and those things are supposed to come into your head.

I didn't want to be with him when he came to this.

I saw it long ago on the hill
in Krug Park while I held two children
and he paced the gravelly road.
Back and forth that Sunday before
he returned to his job.
Drinking left him scattered,
something like the birds
that flew over the park.
I could do nothing
but hold onto the leaves,
the trees, the children.
He had something within him
that brought him to this.
I did not choose to be with him
in that distant day
that NOW when he tired
of flaying the sky
and fell to the ground
on his back, feet kicking,
wings twitching.
I let go of the emptiness
I would always hold.
He used to threaten
he'd drive the car into a tree.
He beat the walls, hurt in his gut.
He'd clap his fists to his chest.
It was no marriage for me.
Even when he was in his
third-floor office
and others envied his position
I saw his movements of despair
night after night.

I moved from his bed,
could not stand the beating wings,
the running feet
the pecking of his beak,
his place with those birds
over Krug Park.

Walker Gallery, Minneapolis

Two chairs lean toward the wall,
one slants forward,
the other back.
The forward one made of yarn,
the backward covered with pins.
No title, but two chairs,
two h's falling
as though part of the alphabet gave way.
A husband yelling in your face.
You lean back,
he leans forward.
No, it's more
when all of that is over,
two h's,
hope and healing.
Not another,
but yourself reaching yourself
saying, *bend,*
forward and backward.
There, in the corner,
a thin woman carrying fruit.
The years didn't hold
but isolated within yourself
you find cause to go on,
this resisting trouble,
sitting it out.
The bundle of silver stars climbs
over your flat house,
playing overhead
with children in the attic,
heat beating from the woodstove
in the corner,
handball and stick ball,
leaning to the other,
one forward
one back.

Swan's Life Span

BOSTON - *A swan will live*
50 years, probably.

Maybe longer in the little bowl of pond,
the baptismal font near the exhaust
and traffic noise of the city.
But what of it?
A swan floating on water,
a distant vapor trail of a plane
in air.
That wedge where shape welcomes
new life
and a lazy street juts off a main artery
and so many shady windows join
transparent hands.
Could it be that all is not lost?
After we are buried under brush for years
someone puts their hand on our heads
to pull us out
and those little words
we have forgotten how to speak
come softy from their bands.

You remember now

you lost mother
and father standing by their beds
fourteen years apart holding their hands
how you lost your love
for your husband and all he had
how your children are grown it's when
you get down
to the barbed wire how traveling in Oregon
the Memaloose Island in the Columbia
River where Indians buried their dead sitting
in the ground you want to be crosslegged
before the fire-sparks rising like pumpkins
thrown in a truck or a turkey as if
it could fly and you could rise above gravity
above the harvested fields
you feel the earth
shrinking under you
pushing you up
the dirt roads
rising behind your car
the country cemeteries
with their grinding stones
the struggle
to get upstream
so hard
even after death
you sit like a skeleton
on Memaloose
still rowing
your canoe
mid-river.

The Transformation Band

Yez I could have washed out
like the Creek County bridge
but Christ redeemers me
the *phlung phlung* of his cross
my Savior the lonesome bundle
of these two worlds he gave me to walk
the sun eating them back to nothing
always nibbling the mowed fields
the worn barns
the pound of my heart when I pass
and there's not much room
but I've been behind so long
yez the angels sing in the winking band
we'll be changed to glory
if praise be true
how the car stumbles over the hill
that long road he took me
more times than I remember
yez Jesus showed how much *luv*
there is in death.

The light of (ado)ration

falls where mostly there was dark and out of dark a small spark, you know a few stars in the sky over the ocean on any given night. You stand on the shore of California. The last light lifts its tongue last off the west coast. And walkers on the beach riffle the sand with their feet and all over you remember what you wish you hadn't said, but the tongue is a road of its own freeway and you hear it sending cars past as you zip your jacket and walk the beach. The dark waves already. Their white lines shoreward you see running toward you like crosswise ropes of lightning. Well that's what the imagination's for. The words you send now from your mouth in (ado)ration bring the ocean's waves. You don't understand how they strike but you feel them across the few yards of beach you have left to walk and how they move toward an onwardness you have seen on the shore of California where it doesn't rain and even less lightnings. But it's not that it never happens but seldom probably, though not being from either coast you don't know. But you know the light is there. You put pressure on the ropes you've seen. The campfires here and there on the beach answering the stars giving back their sameness here on earth.

El Nacimiento

Henrietta Shore
DeSaisset Museum, Santa Clara University, California

Her toes curl under as if hens pecked her feet.
Behind her the gaudy grillwork
of a cemetery. Somebright angels
drifting over the cattlepen

in the turquoise sky. Along the path
there are shadows or pockets of cold
that stick to the skin even on summer nights.
I don't think we choose our way

even the least of us but are shoved
into place and we stick our head
slowly out the door
the mother yelling at us to hurry up.

The tiny *O* of Mary's open mouth
as though Jesus were the hope of the human heart
hands already bound in pulley rope
head crowned with barbed wire.

Indian Beach, Oregon Coast

All the hissing
this landing field
propellers rushing not to be late
anticipation of arrival
the glitter of tide water pushing to shore
unloading butter clams and scallops
seagulls waiting to board white waves
stacked up
even those you see far off
a wave crashes against the standing rock
the cold wind mumbling
you listen as if you were not on course
as if you were not doing something right
they're talking about you
the choices you make
your fundamental right to make them
but you go on with what you think
and watch the squirming field of snakes
you want to say Christ his name rising
on these rows of quonset huts
as if this abundance of waves was his gift
brought to shore
before it rises to the cliffs
and disappears
the thing is to not let go
but to hear the waves with their landing flaps
after the long trip toward land
when you know the ocean ends
and there's no way out
you let down your white water
and you land.

Light Beneath the Skin (or Pronoun 2)

I am holy yours, sweet Christ.
Savior on the road
when I come transfixed.
The blackjam just let out of the jar.
Still a hook in the treetop my love.
Sweet Christ.
I've found nothing else.
Your covering of blood for my heart.
I pack my suitcase
and the garden with asparagus spears in it. The spiked stalks taller each time I look. I pack the black and white linoleum, and all the blood gravy fallen into the cracks. I pack the chicken hearts red and dark as rosebuds. I'm coming, Lord Christ. To be then yours under a lock of trees. Emollients of rain. A sound not yet made by a single lark flying in a treed field. Broken now has to be whole in Christ. I float up the long hallways of rain. Over the waiting shingles. The hard boards of my heart.

The Buzz

Trees clap their hands and out
of intervals that fall,
mulch and the buzzing curb-fire.
But where are the leaves for the next summer?
Will they come from nothing?
From where will their hands clap?
Oh remember how each year they
jump from hard bark--
The sweet buds are doorknobs
for leaves waiting in the branch
to enter the stage and dance
their recital of shade
(stems thin as wands and canes)
until sky divers in transformation,
their parachutes pirouetting
or bees again swarming the awkward hive.

Theology of Deer

The jazz-bows of earth
their roll through space
traveling farther each day
the cherubim on drum
a trumpet of angels
the beats of an old life
when you stop that night on the road through the
Cattaraugus Reserve to watch the northern lights.
The crowd of spirits. Their migration to the rez.
Tuning Indian cars. Holding babies in their arms.
When a deer crosses the road in the fog behind you.
You think Christ for a moment it's him. And you say
dude of dudes and deer of deer.

Stolen Blessing

The moon's a gray pebble in the slingshot \
if \ up over the fence \ someone catch it.
All the insert of new matter \
the interpolation of ancestral claim \ a head-on
inclision of faith \ is all that
(ado)ration is \ a wellspring voice
chugging back and forth \
the pull and drag \ enough to last you all of life.

DIANE GLANCY is Associate Professor at Macalester College in St. Paul where she teaches Native American Literature and Creative Writing. She has received a National Endowment for the Arts, a National Endowment for the Humanities, a Minnesota Book Award and a National Book Award. She received her M.F.A. from the University of Iowa.